An Introduction to Coping with
Stress

2nd Edition

Lee Brosan

ROBINSON

ROBINSON

First published in Great Britain in 2010 by Constable & Robinson Ltd

This edition published in 2018 by Robinson

1 3 5 7 9 10 8 6 4 2

A CIP catalogue record for this book
is available from the British Library.

Important note
This book is not intended as a substitute for medical advice
or treatment. Any person with a condition requiring medical
attention should consult a qualified medical practitioner
or suitable therapist.

ISBN: 978-1-47214-019-7

Typeset in Bembo by Initial Typesetting Services, Edinburgh
Printed and bound in Great Britain by Clays Ltd, St Ives plc

Papers used by Robinson are from well-managed forests
and other responsible sources.

Robinson
An imprint of
Little, Brown Book Group
Carmelite House
50 Victoria Embankment
London EC4Y 0DZ

An Hachette UK Company
www.hachette.co.uk
www.littlebrown.co.uk

Contents

Acknowledgements

I am indebted to Gillian Todd, my co-author on *Overcoming Stress*, for her help in developing many of the ideas written about here. I am also very grateful to Nicola Ridgeway for introducing me to the idea of the Resourceful Self, which is mentioned briefly at the end.

About This Book

Most of us feel stressed at some point in our lives, and find things difficult to cope with. Stress is so much part of our normal existence that sometimes we just take this for granted. For some people the problem remains fairly manageable, though for others it can start to take over their lives. This book should be able to offer some help to all.

This book is based on the ideas and techniques of cognitive behavioural therapy (CBT), which is an effective way of tackling a whole range of difficulties. Part 1 describes the symptoms of stress, and talks about how it starts and what keeps it going, and how thoughts play a role in this process. Part 2 looks at the practical skills that you can use to combat the symptoms of stress, including how to tackle the thoughts that contribute to it.

Many people will find it most helpful to read and work through the book from start to finish. You may prefer, however, just to dip into the parts that seem most relevant to you. It's often helpful to write things down, and Part 2 contains several exercises to guide you.

This book is designed for you to use on your own, or with a friend or partner. But if you find that you're not making progress, or that your problems seem too overwhelming to tackle in this way, don't despair. Go to your family doctor and talk about alternatives. Medication or help from a therapist can make all the difference.

Good luck!

Lee Brosan

Part 1: ABOUT STRESS

Nicky has just moved with her family to a new town. The house that they've bought needs a lot of building work carried out to make it habitable, and the builders they've chosen are very unreliable. Nicky is finding it more and more difficult to cope, and finds herself bursting into tears and shouting at the builders, who are then more likely to disappear. She feels completely powerless and inadequate.

Greg has been working for his company for two years, and has just been moved to a new position. It's a promotion, but he is spending at least two and a half hours a day in heavy traffic to get to his new team. He is incredibly frustrated at the waste of his time, and is starting to get very bad pains in his stomach and his back, and is drinking far too much when he gets home in the evening.

Mary's elderly mother is ill, and she has come to stay. She was always quite demanding, but illness has made her much more so. She spends her whole time asking Mary to do things for her, even things that she could do herself. Mary can't make her see that she still has other commitments apart from her, and finds herself getting more and more frustrated and upset.

1

What Is Stress?

Stress is a very common experience, and is the way in which we respond to demands that are made of us by other people, or even by ourselves. We may feel overburdened at work, feel out of control of the number of things we have to tackle at once, or feel that if we don't manage everything then we've failed. For some of us stress remains at a fairly manageable level, but for others it can become much more severe, and may start to interfere with the way that they can function, or affect their physical well-being.

It can be helpful to think of stress in terms of the four different ways it can affect us.

The effect on our emotions

Stress can affect how we feel inside. We may react to stress by feeling:

- irritable

- tense, agitated, restless

- weepy, tearful

- sad, despondent.

The effect on our thoughts

Stress can affect how we think about ourselves and what is happening to us. Typical stress-related thoughts include:

> '*I can't cope, this is too difficult for me.*'

> '*I've just got too much to do; I'll never be able to get everything done and if I don't, something will go disastrously wrong.*'

> '*It's not fair, these sort of things don't happen to other people.*'

> '*I'm such a failure, I'll never be able to sort this out.*'

The effect on our bodies

When we're stressed we may notice the following physical signs:

- the need to breathe faster to increase oxygen in the body

- muscular aches and pains

- headaches, backaches

- stomach aches, indigestion, heartburn, constipation or diarrhoea

- problems with breathing, or with our hearts

- problems with our skin, such as eczema or rashes.

The effect on our behaviour

It's quite usual to behave slightly differently from normal when we're feeling stressed. Common stress-related behaviour includes:

- losing our tempers

- drinking or eating or smoking too much

- running away or avoiding the difficult situation

- overreacting to a situation

- being in a constant rush.

If these sound familiar to you, then it's likely that you may be experiencing problems with stress. You may not experience all of them, and people vary widely in the types of problems and symptoms they experience, but these are the kind of things to look out for.

Are you stressed?

So, are you stressed? Well, you probably are at least a bit. You have picked up this book after all. Given that life is quite complex and demanding, most of us are stressed at some point in the day or week, and have bad days when we feel that we just can't cope. But there are a few questions you can ask yourself to see if it could be a bit more than that for you.

- Do you feel stressed most of the time, and are the bad days turning into bad weeks or bad months?

- Is feeling stressed affecting your ability to carry out your normal activities?

- Is your health being affected by stress?

- Are your relationships being affected by how stressed you feel?

This book will be helpful to anyone experiencing any level of stress, but if you've answered 'yes' to one or more of these questions, you should find the strategies contained within it particularly helpful.

What is stress?

The central idea about stress is that it's how we respond when we're under pressure – even when the pressure is coming from demands that we place on ourselves. But stress is not just about pressure – it's also about how we view it and cope with it. People differ greatly in the extent to which they feel that they can cope with the pressure that they are under. Faced with the same situation, one person may feel that they are able to manage it well, while another may feel completely overwhelmed.

Stress – a definition

Stress is what we experience when we feel that the demands or pressures on us are greater than we think we can cope with. Stress affects our thoughts, feelings, bodies and behaviour.

We talk about the situation that makes us feel stressed as the *stressor*, and the response we have to it as *stress*.

2

How the Way We Think Affects
Our Stress Levels

As we'll see below, feelings and thinking are so linked that one way in which we can learn to manage our feelings is to think about our thinking, which plays an extremely important role in stress.

To demonstrate this, imagine that your partner is away and you're lying in bed at night when you hear a rattle at the back door. What goes through your mind? You might think someone was trying to break in and rob or hurt you. Or you might think that the cat flap was blocked and the cat couldn't get in. Or you might think that your partner had come back early and lost their key. In each case, the situation – the sound at the back door – was the same, but the thoughts that you had about it were different.

Furthermore, it's not just the thoughts that would be different, but the feelings that go with them. If you thought that someone was trying to break in you would be very frightened, but if you thought it was the cat you probably wouldn't be, and would feel OK, or possibly a bit irritated. Similarly, if it was your partner returning home you might feel pleased.

So the way in which you *think* about things makes a major difference to how you *feel* about them.

Two kinds of thought are important in stress:

• the way that we weigh up the situation that creates the stress (the stressor)

• the way in which we weigh up our ability to cope with it.

These are not always conscious thoughts, and they are often complicated, but they play a big part in how stressed we feel. Learning to identify them can make a big difference to how stressed we feel, and we'll talk more about this in Part 2.

3

What Keeps Stress Going?

Identifying our thoughts isn't, however, the end of the story.

What we do can also make a big difference to how we feel about what's causing us stress and our ability to cope with it. If we behave in a way that we're pleased with, and manage to get to grips with the problematic situation, we'll be much more likely to see the situations and ourselves in a more positive light. As a result, our thoughts will become more positive and we'll feel much less stressed. We'll get back to 'normal'. But if the way that we react makes things worse, or we feel that we have failed, then our negative thoughts will get more extreme and we'll feel more stressed. Nicky's story illustrates how this can happen. (Note, we're using 'cope' here to mean whatever we do in the situation, even if it doesn't feel like coping!)

We can see how this happens in the diagram opposite. At the top and on the right-hand side of the diagram are the thoughts that lead to stress. On the left-hand side is what we do to cope, which can either make things better or make them worse.

Trigger or stressor

(the situation or events that make us feel stressed)

Thoughts about the situation

Thoughts about our ability to cope

How we feel

What we do

Nicky's story

Nicky is juggling her children and a part-time job as well as trying to cope with the builders.

Trigger: Pick children up and go home. It's obvious the builders haven't been here all day even though they promised that they would make the kitchen usable by the end of the week. Washing machine still not plumbed in.

Thoughts about the situation: This is so annoying. They promised they'd do it. I can't stand another weekend in the freezing cold with no hot water and no proper cooking and washing facilities. They'll never finish in time now.

Thoughts about my ability to cope: I ought to be able to ring them up, but they never take any notice of me and just fob me off with excuses. I'm so pathetic.

How I feel: Upset, furious.

What I do: Start trying to make supper in the microwave, but in such a state that I knock the stew over into the plaster dust, and we don't have anything to eat. Snap at the children when they ask what's for supper.

Thoughts about my ability to cope get worse: I really am useless, I can't cope, I'm such a dreadful mother – it's not their fault, why won't anyone help me . . . ?

Stress gets worse . . .

The way in which Nicky responded to stress made a big difference to how she felt about herself and the situation. What could she have thought differently that might have made things better? We'll look at that in the next chapter.

Four Important Facts About Stress

1 Stress is not all in the mind

We have talked a lot about thinking. Are we saying that stress is all in the mind? The answer to this is absolutely not. People do lead very stressful lives in this day and age. Most of us have a great deal to cope with, and need to juggle work, families, finances, unemployment, housing problems, travel problems – the list is endless. But by understanding the kind of thoughts that we have about this we can find ways to better tackle things.

2 Stress is normal

The fact that you're feeling stressed does not mean that there's something 'wrong' with you. Sometimes you might feel that you're going mad, or that you're the only person in the world who can't cope. It's easy to compare yourself with other people and think that they are doing OK and you're not. But as a character in a novel by the author Marian Keyes said: 'The trouble with us is that we compare our insides with other people's outsides.' It's quite possible that half the people you meet think you're doing brilliantly and it's only them who can't cope!

3 Excitement is not stress

Life is not *all* stress – we can also feel positively challenged, excited or happy. Some people use the term 'eustress' (literally, 'good stress') to describe this. While recognising that these states exist (if you're lucky!) it does not seem sensible to describe them in terms of stress, and so in this book we're looking at more troubling aspects of stress that we need to learn to cope with.

4 Not all negative emotions are stress

Human beings have a whole range of different emotions, some good, some bad. Common 'bad' emotions are things like anxiety, depression or anger, and some people use the term 'stress' when they are talking about any of these. To complicate things, stress often does include aspects of these emotions. But when anxiety or depression are very extreme, they need to be understood in their own right. If you think that you, or someone close to you, may be suffering from one of these conditions, then it would be sensible to go and see your family doctor, who will be able to help you decide exactly what is wrong with you, and will help you find the right kind of help.

Part 2: COPING WITH STRESS

There's a range of things that have been found to be effective in helping to tackle stress, which we'll now look at. You don't need to read all of them to get the benefit but it may be helpful to look at the next chapter, which talks about how to deal with your thoughts, because thoughts form such an important part of the stress process.

Using Your Thoughts to Help Combat Stress

We know that when we're stressed it's easy to think in a very negative way. There's a vicious circle that can make our stress worse and worse, which looks like this:

Stressful   Stressed
thoughts   mood

Very often, our stressful thoughts are also rather unfair and unrealistic. They are unfair in the sense that we tend to see the worst in everything, and ignore aspects of the situation that might not be so bad. We forget that we have managed to deal with things like this before. They are also unrealistic in the sense that thinking is often based on guesswork and exaggeration, rather than on carefully weighing things up. We call these *stressful automatic thoughts*, or SATs, because very often they just pop into our heads fully formed, without us weighing up whether they are the best way of seeing things.

There are a number of common ways in which our stressful automatic thoughts can be thought of as biased or distorted. We sometimes refer to these as thinking 'errors'.

Thinking errors and stressful automatic thoughts

Have a look through the list of SATs below and see if you can identify some errors that you use. The list doesn't include every single way that thoughts can be biased and unfair, so you may be aware of others too. But it's important to ask yourself the following question: How can thoughts based on such faulty logic be true?!

Filtering

Seeing only the bad and ignoring the good. You might forget or ignore good things, and concentrate only on the bad – you see your problems and weaknesses but disregard your strengths and accomplishments.

Overgeneralisation ☐

If one thing goes wrong, you think that means everything else is wrong too. If you have difficulty with one friend, that means no one likes you. If you overcook the potatoes, that means the whole meal is ruined.

Blowing things out of proportion or catastrophising ☐

If you make one small error, then it means that something terrible will happen as a result. If you're late for a meeting, you think your boss will be furious and you'll end up getting sacked.

Black-and-white, or all-or-nothing thinking ☐

You see things as either completely good or completely bad, with no middle ground. If you don't score 100 per cent on a test, you must be really stupid. If you're not the best at a game, you're rubbish at it.

Labelling ☐

This means talking about yourself or others in a critical way, and calling yourself names – 'I'm stupid'; 'I'm incompetent'; 'he's a sexist swine'. You feel the labels sum up you and others, and there's nothing else to you.

Mind reading

You believe that you know what others are thinking – usually bad. It's about you, and it's negative. You end up reacting to what you *think* other people are thinking, without finding out what they really *are* thinking.

Fortune telling

You imagine the way things might go in the future – normally badly – and respond emotionally as if this is really what's going to happen, when in fact you probably don't have a clue!

Discounting the positive

If good things do happen, you find a way of saying they don't count. 'I know I dealt with that OK, but anyone could have done.' 'She only said my report was good because she didn't want to upset me.'

Personalisation

If something bad happens, it must have been your fault, or aimed at you. 'It always rains when I plan picnics.'

Shoulds and oughts

You spend a lot of time thinking about what you *should* do, or how the world *ought* to be. But what you're doing here is imposing very unrealistic demands on yourself and the world. And then feel very bad when neither you nor the world measure up.

Three-step plan to overcome stressful thinking

Step 1: Recognise your stressful thoughts

REMINDER

SATs are stressful automatic thoughts – thoughts that just pop into our heads without us considering whether or not they are accurate or justified.

Because SATs are so automatic, we tend to just accept them as facts, and don't even realise that we're having them. The first step in learning to overcome them is to recognise that we're having them. A good way to do this is to fill out a 'SATs record' like the one shown on page 25, for a week.

Make your own SATs record in a notebook or on a computer to carry out this exercise.

Every time you notice you're getting stressed, write down:

- The date and time

- The situation that you're in – what has happened to make you feel stressed

- SATs – exactly what was going through your mind about the situation

- The emotion that you feel.

You could rate this on a scale of 0 to 10 (10 is the worst) so that you will be able to remember how strongly you felt.

TIP

Identifying SATs

Try to write things down as soon as you notice that you're feeling more stressed. If you wait, it'll be harder to remember exactly what you were thinking.

Ask yourself:

- What does the situation mean to me?
- What am I afraid may happen?
- What does it say about my ability to cope?
- What does it say about my life or my future?
- What does it say about me as a person?
- What does it say about other people?

Keep this record for a week, and at the end of the week look at your stressful thoughts. Do you notice that there are similar ideas that keep cropping up? Look at the list of thinking errors on pages 19–22 and notice if you're making any of them. Watch out for the same error coming up again and again.

_____

_____

_____

_____

Remember Nicky's story? Opposite is an example from the SATs record she kept for a week.

STRESSFUL AUTOMATIC THOUGHT RECORD

Date	Situation	Stressful Automatic Thoughts	Stressful Emotion
	Where you are, what's going on around you	Exactly what was going through your mind. Record thought, and if you like, try to classify the thinking error	Describe emotion and rate how strongly you feel it (0–10)
Monday pm	Got home with girls. Builders haven't been here.	I can't cope with another weekend without heating or cooking or hot water. The builders would never do this if my husband dealt with them. They know they don't need to take any notice of me because I'm so pathetic and inadequate.	Upset, angry, tearful. 8

Step 2: Questioning and challenging your SATs and learning to think in a more fair and realistic way

Once you've identified your SATs, you can learn how to question them, and how to examine the situation from a more objective viewpoint.

- Notice the thinking errors that you're making, and ask yourself how something can be true if it's based on such faulty reasoning.

- Think about the situation, and a more fair and realistic alternative. This can be like having an argument with yourself, or pretending that you're in court and have to prove that the evidence really backs up your view. Fight the stressful thoughts by trying to come up with fair and realistic alternatives.

- Reassess how you feel when you've been able to come up with alternatives. Do things seem a bit less bad? Do you feel a bit less stressed?

These questions should help you think of ways to challenge your thoughts. Read through them and use them to tackle your thoughts.

Questions to ask to help challenge thoughts

- What is the evidence for the way you are thinking? Is there any?

- What is the evidence that goes against the way you are thinking?

- What would be a more fair and realistic way of thinking about the situation? Is there an alternative to your view?

- What would other people say? Would they agree that the evidence supports your thoughts? If not, what would they say? What would you say to a friend who said they were thinking as you do? Would you agree with them?

- How would someone else react to this situation? Ask around and find out.

- Are you setting yourself unreasonable standards?

- Are you forgetting relevant facts?

- Are you thinking in all-or-nothing terms?

- Or catastrophising?

- Are you underestimating how well you can deal with this problem, or have dealt with similar ones in the past?

- Are you setting unrealistic standards for yourself or other people?

- What if this happens? Would it really be so bad? Are you reading the future and assuming it's bad?

- How will you think about this situation in a week's time? Will you still be worrying?

- How about in a year? Is it really worth the amount of stress it's causing you?

Challenging your thoughts isn't easy, and it takes practice. Just as nobody gets fit by going to the gym once, nobody can completely change themselves by challenging their thoughts once. But the more you do it, the easier it will get, and the more psychologically fit your thoughts will be!

Use the SATs challenging record to help you.

_____

_____

_____

_____

_____

_____

This is how Nicky learnt to challenge her thoughts.

			SATS CHALLENGING RECORD		
Date	Situation	SATS	Emotion	Fair and Realistic Thought	Emotion
Monday pm	Got home with girls. Builders haven't been here.	I can't cope with another weekend without heating or cooking or hot water. The builders would never do this if my husband dealt with them. They know they don't need to take any notice of me because I'm so pathetic and inadequate.	upset, angry, tearful.	I think I'm mindreading and personalising. Everyone says builders are unreliable because they take on too many jobs at once, so I don't need to blame myself. It's a pain, but maybe we could go out for supper, or even persuade Neil to take us to a hotel for the weekend!	Much calmer; looking forward to going out.

Step 3: Acting on your new thoughts

Now that you're able to identify thoughts that are less stress-inducing, and which are more fair and realistic, the next step is to take action. Ask yourself what you can do differently now that you're thinking in a more realistic way. For instance, if you're less worried that your boss will sack you if you can't do everything perfectly and fit everything in, then you could pluck up the courage to go and ask for help. If you're less pessimistic about exercising because you're so bad at it, then make a start and see how you feel!

Our behaviour is an extremely powerful tool in helping us to feel differently. Once we start to change our behaviour, we give ourselves very powerful messages that we *can* cope – because we've seen that we can, we don't just have to tell ourselves that we can!

Use the new way of thinking to work out how you're going to change what you do, and you will be amazed at how different things can be!

6

Combating Stress in Your Body

For each symptom listed in the table below, rate how much you're experiencing the problem at the moment.

Physical symptoms of stress

0 *You don't have a problem with that symptom at the moment*
1 *You have it in a mild or moderate way; it's not there all the time and it's not too bad when it is*
2 *You have the symptom most of the time, and it's very troubling for you*

MUSCLES AND JOINTS	SCORE (0, 1 or 2)
Tension and pain	
Neck and shoulder pain	
Backache	
Headache	
TOTAL SCORE:	

Physical symptoms of stress continued

0   *You don't have a problem with that symptom at the moment*

1   *You have it in a mild or moderate way; it's not there all the time and it's not too bad when it is*

2   *You have the symptom most of the time, and it's very troubling for you*

STOMACH	SCORE (0, 1 or 2)
Indigestion	
Vomiting	
Heartburn	
Constipation	
Diarrhoea	
Irritable bowel	
Flatulence	
TOTAL SCORE:	
HEART	
Palpitations	
Heart missing a beat	
Angina	
Pain	
TOTAL SCORE:	

BREATHING	SCORE (0, 1 or 2)
Shortness of breath	
Breathing too rapidly (hyperventilation)	
TOTAL SCORE:	
SEXUAL	
No sex drive	
Impotence	
Heavy menstrual periods	
Absence of menstrual periods	
TOTAL SCORE:	
SKIN	
Spots	
Rashes	
Eczema	
Allergic reactions	
TOTAL SCORE:	
GENERAL	
More frequent colds and flu	
Allergies	
Low energy	
Restlessness	
TOTAL SCORE:	
GRAND TOTAL:	

Your score on the chart is how badly you're being physically affected by stress at the moment (unless you have another physical or mental condition that would explain the symptoms). Add others if the list doesn't include symptoms you know are stress-related for you. Make a note of your score. When you've been carrying out some of the coping strategies you should see it improve!

How does stress affect our bodies?

When we feel stressed, our bodies produce a number of hormones – the best known of which is adrenaline – and chemical messengers that spark off what is known as the 'fight or flight' response. The adrenaline causes a lot of changes that are all designed to make us faster and stronger. It also makes our senses keener and makes us much less sensitive to pain. It can also make us very attuned to the source of danger.

All this is extremely useful when the danger that faces us is physical and we need to respond to it with speed and strength. Sometimes the problems that we're facing today need a different kind of response, but the fight or flight response can still be very useful, gearing us up to respond quickly and efficiently in troubled situations. Once we have confronted and dealt with the danger, then the fight or flight response dies down and we get back to normal.

The problems arise when the stress goes on and on, and our bodies don't have a chance to return to normal. To keep going, our bodies need to 'borrow' physical resources from normal bodily functions such as eating and digestion, the activity of the immune system or the reproductive system. This means that if stress goes on for a long time, these functions start to show the strain. We get aches and pains in our muscles; our stomachs start playing up; our skin starts getting spots and rashes; and we pick up bugs and colds more easily because our immune system is affected. In women, the menstrual cycle can stop or be very disrupted.

To add to the difficulty, these pains and physical problems then become something else in our lives that we have to cope with, and add to the pressure that we're under. It's much harder to cope with an important presentation at work when you're doubled up with stomach ache, and much harder to meet new people when you're covered in spots!

Helping your body to relax

Learning to relax can help to counteract the fight or flight response when it is no longer needed. It can help to calm us down mentally too.

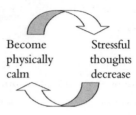

Become
physically
calm

Stressful
thoughts
decrease

Often stress starts to build up in our bodies before we really notice it, until it makes itself felt through illness and pain. We spend a lot of time with our bodies scrunched up, our shoulders hunched, our muscles tense and our fists clenched. So one way in which you can help yourself is to be aware of what your body is doing. When you wake up in the morning, stretch your arms and legs and back and neck – don't force the stretch, but just let your body loosen and expand. As you go through the day, check your body from time to time. Ask yourself:

* Are you holding your muscles tight?

* Is your body contorted as you hunch over the computer?

- Are you walking around with your shoulders raised around your ears?

- Are you ignoring the fact that you're thirsty or hungry?

- Are you bending or lifting in ways that hurt your body?

If you notice that you're doing these things, then just take a moment to allow your body to return to its natural position, and let the tension drain out of your body.

Making these small steps can make big changes to your body. But make sure that being aware of your body doesn't mean homing in on its imperfections. You may not be a six-foot muscle man or a size-eight model, but you can still be OK!

Many people find that exercise helps enormously to release physical stress. Others find that yoga is extremely helpful, particularly since it combines physical and mental techniques. Meditation is another method that seems to work well. Still other people buy one of the many relaxation CDs that are commercially available – look for ones that talk about *progressive muscular relaxation*, which has been shown to be very effective in aiding relaxation.

Exercising

Unless you're naturally keen on sport, starting to build a sensible exercise regime can be very difficult. Most of us need to become generally more active in our daily lives as well as doing some vigorous exercise two or three times a week.

Increasing your daily activities

• Think about your daily life, and see if there are any adjustments that you can make. Can you get to work in a different way? Can you drive to the Park and Ride and walk into town? Or bike? Can you get off the bus one stop earlier than you need to? Can you find a nice flight of stairs and make yourself go up and down it for fifteen minutes? Can you persuade your children that they really want to go and kick a football with you for half an hour instead of watching TV? If you can increase your daily activity in these ways then you're doing extremely well.

Formal exercise

• In addition to being more active generally, your physical well-being will improve if you can do some kind of vigorous exercise two or three times a week for perhaps twenty or thirty minutes. Think about what kind of activity you might like to do. Do you enjoy being part of a team or exercising on your own? Do you have good hand–eye coordination that would mean ball games would be for you, or have you always secretly wondered if you could run a marathon if you trained for one? Do you love being in the country and find indoor sports miss the point? Try to find something that will give you a sense of pleasure, or at least have some aspect to it that will make up for the pain. If you don't enjoy it at all, you won't do it. Filling in the activity table like the one on page 40 might help you to get started.

Making changes

Make a plan for what you'd like to do differently to cope with physical aspects of stress. Make sure your plan is:

- *realistic* – don't plan to run the marathon if you can't even run for the bus yet

- *specific* – say exactly what you're going to do, and when you're going to do it

• *measurable* – make sure that you have a way of being able to keep track of what you're doing. This might mean using a step counter to count the number of steps you take a day, or timing a run for ten minutes.

Remember Greg, who was becoming very physically stressed? This is what he came up with to help combat the stress:

ACTIVITY TABLE		
	What I plan to do	**When I am going to do it**
Daily Activity	Leave car at Park and Ride and walk a mile.	Every day – getting to work and going back to car.
Vigorous Exercise	Phone Mick and see if he can play squash/join squash club.	Tuesday and Friday evenings.
Relaxation	Use time in car to practise mindfulness.	As soon as I notice I'm getting stressed!

Eating sensibly

Many people find that eating helps them to calm down and stop feeling stressed. Nevertheless, we need to be careful about what we're eating and how often we eat to 'de-stress'. Often this can involve binging or over-eating. It almost always involves 'comfort' food that's high in fat and sugar rather than healthier options. If we do it too often, we're likely to put on weight. We're also likely to stop eating healthy foods that keep our bodies functioning well, and thus add to problems of digestion, gaining weight, spots, etc. Try using the techniques set out in this book, which will provide you with a much healthier way of 'de-stressing' – and you won't get the guilt afterwards!

Remember that the principles of a good diet are to eat less fatty foods, and less sugar and salt. Our diets should include a lot of dietary fibre, wholegrain cereals and pulses, and lots of fresh vegetables and fruit, as well as good-quality protein in lean meat and fish. Think about small changes that you could make and start to introduce them slowly. They will soon become incorporated into your diet without it seeming like a radical change. Experiment with cooking methods so that you can enjoy the new foods.

Drinking sensibly

This is very difficult if you're someone who's used to opening a bottle as soon as you get home after a day's work and doubly difficult because alcohol is so effective in the short term, but try to remember government guidelines – no more than 14 units a week for women and men. If you regularly drink as much as 14 units, this should be spread over three or more days. Make sure that you're aware of the alcohol content of your drinks and keep a close eye on what you're doing. Think of things that you could do instead of drinking. Go and have a bath if the temptation overwhelms you, or go out for a walk, until the urge to keep drinking starts to wear off. Experiment with non-alcoholic drinks that will fool you into thinking you've drunk something – tonic water with ice and lemon, or fizzy water with angostura bitters.

Smoking

A great deal has been written about the harmful effects of smoking. It's not just that it can have life-threatening effects on your body but that generally it has negative effects on your health in a day-to-day way, and this can make it more difficult to cope with other pressures. Giving up smoking can be very stressful in the short term, but there are long-term benefits that should make the effort worthwhile. It means that you don't have to worry about whether you're harming yourself physically, and as you become more fit you're likely to feel mentally better too. Although it's difficult to stop smoking, there's a lot of help available now, and your family doctor or pharmacist should be able to talk to you about what would be best for you.

You may be able to choose other ways of reducing stress, such as meditation or exercise, which could have very beneficial effects.

Making changes

Decide what changes you would like to make to your eating and drinking habits. Make a plan and, like the activity table we've just looked at, set reasonable, specific and measurable goals.

For each of these tables, make a plan for the week ahead. Then at the end of every day write down what you've managed to do. At the end of the week, have a look and see how it's gone. If you've stuck to your plan, then hooray! Give yourself a big reward. If not, then think about whether the plans you made were a bit too hard, or a bit too vague, and make a more realistic one to try the next week.

GREG'S PLAN		
	What I plan to do	**When I am going to do it**
Eating	Have healthy snacks in the car instead of stopping for chocolate – boiled eggs/ cheese/pears.	Every day.
Drinking	I'll have a beer when I get home, but then stop after one!!	Every day.
Relaxation	Use time in car to practise mindfulness.	As soon as I notice I'm getting stressed!

7

Identifying Sources of Stress

Sometimes it's all too easy to identify what is causing you stress. This is especially true if you've suffered a major life event in the past few months. This would be something like getting divorced, losing your job or having someone close to you die.

Sources of stress

- death of a partner

- divorce or separation

- jail term

- death of a close family member

- personal injury or illness

- loss of your job

- moving house

- retirement

- serious illness of a family member

- new child

- change of job

- money problems

- death of a close friend.

However, sometimes the things that cause stress are not major events but smaller difficulties. These could be a combination of problems in different areas, such as your children having problems at school, traffic jams on the way to work, noisy neighbours, fights about the washing-up, a messy house . . . the list is endless! It can be much harder to notice because we tend to accept them as part of our daily lives. These 'hassles' might not be so noticeable as major life events, but they can affect us just as much.

In the table opposite, make a list of all the things that are causing you stress. Include both major events and small hassles.

THINGS THAT MAKE ME FEEL STRESSED	HOW STRESSED IT MAKES ME FEEL (0–100)

8

Seven Steps to Dealing with Problems

For every problem under the sun
There is a remedy, or there is none;
If there be one, try and find it
If there be none, never mind it.

Anon

Once you've identified the problem that's making you stressed, you need to find the best way to cope with it.

Step 1: Decide which problem to tackle first

Looking at the list of problems that are making you feel stressed, think about each one, and decide which would be good to tackle first. This may be the one that's causing you most stress, or it may be one that's easiest to make progress with. Choose one that you can start work on right away – don't worry

about the others because you can come back to
them later.

Step 2: Set goals

Set goals for the problem. How would you like
things to turn out? How can you make that come
about? Make sure your goals are:

- *realistic* – the goal is reasonable, not something
  that's unlikely ever to happen, no matter who
  was doing it

- *specific* – you can say exactly what you're trying to achieve

- *measurable* – you'll know when you've done
  it.

Set a time for when you will have achieved the
goal, or achieved the first steps towards it. Make
this specific too – 'next Wednesday' is better than
'sometime next month'.

Step 3: Think about your resources

Think about your strengths and your resources.
Have you been able to solve similar problems in the
past? Have you got personal strengths that made it

easier? Are there other people who might be able to help you? (They wouldn't solve the problem for you but rather help you to solve the problem yourself, or give you support while you do so.)

_____

_____

_____

_____

_____

Step 4: Think about solutions

Next, think about things you could do that might help in this situation, and write down as many ideas as you possibly can. Don't worry if some of them seem crazy or if they won't solve the problem completely – just write them down.

_____

_____

_____

_____

_____

Think about the pros and cons of each solution you've written down, and think about whether you have the strengths and resources to carry them out. You don't have to solve the problem completely – just start to move in the right direction.

Choose a solution!

Step 5: Make an action plan

What can you do to bring about your goal? Do you usually try to cope in one way when another would really be better? Can you shift to a different way of coping that might fit the situation better? Make a plan for how you might start to achieve the goal. Remember that a journey of a thousand miles begins with a single step, and make sure that your plan includes small manageable steps, not massive, unrealistic ones. For instance, if you want to get fit but have taken no exercise for two years, don't plan to start by spending two hours a day in the gym.

Step 6: Carry out your plan!

Now that you've made your plan, don't let anything put you off! Just start with the first small step.

Step 7: Review your progress

Once a week sit down and review your progress. Is your action plan working? Are you getting closer to your goals? Do you feel less stressed? Do you need to make changes in your action plan to make it more effective or because you've reached a new phase of the problem?

9

Managing Your Time

- Are you often late for appointments and meetings?

- Do you miss deadlines?

- Do you agree to do things when you really don't want to?

- Do you have trouble deciding what to do first?

Sometimes the problem with stress is that we just have too many things to do. As a colleague once said, 'When I get stressed, it's not that any of the things I have to deal with are really too difficult for me, it's just that I have to deal with them all at once.' It's really important that we learn how to manage our time as well as we possibly can.

Before we start thinking about details of how to manage our time, we need to ask ourselves what we want to use time for. We need to be clear about our values and our priorities, so that we can make sure that the way in which we spend our time is meaningful for us.

Think about the different areas of your life: work, family, friends, interests, health and finances. What is important to you? What makes your heart sing? Make sure that the way that you spend your time reflects these values. Of course, sometimes you have to do things that don't conform to this. Washing-up rarely makes anyone's heart sing but it may be a small part of looking after your family, which could well be an important area for you.

Remember that rest and relaxation, spending time with family and friends, or even watching TV, can be important, high-priority activities if they are part of your larger values.

To see how you're doing, spend one or two days reviewing how you actually use your time. In the box opposite, write down everything that you did. In the next column, write down how long you spent on it. Try to make this as accurate as possible. In the third column, you're going to rate according to how much of a priority it was.

A This was a priority and was a good use of time
B This wasn't a priority in terms of values, but it was necessary
C This was neither important nor necessary – I was wasting time when I knew I should have been doing something else

WHAT I DID	HOW LONG	CODE

• Do the activities in your box reflect a good mix of As and Bs without too many Cs? Are you spending your time doing the things that you know are important to you? If not, then a new plan may be in order!

Four steps to time management

Step 1: Whenever you have too many things to do, and are getting panicked and muddled about how to cope, give yourself ten minutes to think before you start to act. Make a list of everything that you have to do.

Step 2: Think about what order you need to do things in. What's necessary? What's important? Are you putting some things off because they feel too difficult and are therefore making life more problematic? Are you pretending that easy things are important? Go back to your priorities and decide in what order you really should do things. Be realistic – don't include everything on your list for the day when you know that you won't be able to do it all.

Step 3: Get a system for labelling your list. Use different colour highlighters, or mark each item with a number or letter, or rewrite the list in the order you've decided to do things in. Put an asterisk by the really important things.

Step 4: Start on your list! As you get things done, tick them off on the list – it will help to feel that you're coping well!

Saying 'no'

One of the problems about trying to organise your time is that very often things will get sprung on you by other people. Sometimes you'll want to do what you're asked and have time for it, but at many other times it will be problematic. You may feel that the person has no right to ask you for yet another favour, or that you'd like to help but just don't have the time.

Perhaps a neighbour has asked you to pick their child up from school when you were planning to take your own children out for a treat. Maybe your boss has come in with a deadline that you've no hope of completing. Whatever the cause, you will be able to manage your own time much better if you can learn to say 'no'.

If the mere prospect of learning to do this fills you with apprehension, go back to the SATs lists on pages 19–22 and ask yourself what underlies the feeling. Are you worried that if you say 'no' your friend won't like you or won't ask your children to parties? Are you worried that your boss will think you're a skiver? Do you feel morally obliged to put other people first? Use the forms to come up with fair and reasonable responses to the SATs. It will be much easier to learn to say 'no' if you believe that you have the right to do it.

Four steps to saying 'no'

Step 1: Remember that your rights are as important as everyone else's. If the request is unreasonable, or if you don't have time, or if you would have to make unwelcome changes to your own plans, you have the right to say 'no'.

Step 2: Explain clearly that you're not able to help, and give short reasons why. Say 'no'. Don't get angry or upset, even if the other person doesn't like it. It may be difficult for them if they are used to you saying 'yes', and they will have to adapt to the change. Remember you have the right to say 'no'!

Step 3: If the other person doesn't want to accept your refusal, and keeps coming up with objections to your reasons, think of yourself as an old-fashioned vinyl record that's broken and got stuck. Just keep sticking to your point. Once you've explained, you don't have to go into it again – just keep repeating that you can't help. Try 'I'm sorry, I would have liked to help, but I've explained my decision and I need to stick to it.'

Step 4: Practise different ways of saying 'no'. 'I'm afraid not'. . . 'that won't be possible'. . . 'I won't be able to make that'. . . 'that's not going to be possible'. Practise in the mirror so you can make sure you look convincing!

Be careful about saying 'yes'

Sometimes we're asked to do things that we really do want to do, and we say 'yes'. Nevertheless, even when we want to do something we need to be careful.

One danger is referred to as the 'elephant on the horizon'. If someone asks you to do something that's a long way in the future you say 'yes'. You would like to give a talk at that important seminar. You would like to chair the committee next year, or organise the village flower festival. As long as it's far enough in the future it seems fine. But, like the elephant, the closer it gets the bigger it grows, and not just bigger but also more scary. When things are some distance away, you see the attractive side much more clearly. The closer it gets, however, the more the attractions recede, and the more and more visible the scary side gets. Make sure you know what you're letting yourself in for.

Make sure that you have time. Sometimes someone will ask you to do something that you really want to do, and you don't let yourself think about whether or not you have enough time to do it. If you're going to say 'yes', you will have to plan carefully. Is there something less important that you can give up? Are you prepared for your life to be very busy, and perhaps having to work extremely hard, or sacrificing another area of your life?

TIP

Managing your time

- Make lists
- Choose things according to your priorities
- Plan carefully – daily, weekly, monthly, even six-monthly
- Get to know your body clock – if you function better in the morning, plan to do difficult things then. If you're better later in the evening, then plan to do things at that time
- Delegate – ask family members to share the household chores that they can
- Keep your goals in mind
- Break projects down into manageable chunks
- Get organised – it's possible to waste a huge amount of time because you can't find things, or your space is badly organised. It's definitely worth spending time sorting out clutter and mess in the long run
- Build in breaks and leisure time
- Look at a day as a series of time slots, and plan accordingly

10

Decluttering

'How come my wardrobe is packed but I don't have anything to wear?'

'I'm meant to be finishing my report but I can't find any of the papers.'

'I can't stand all the mess in here!'

'I can never find anything!'

If these sound familiar, then the problem is clutter – the accumulation of bits and pieces that you never quite put away or get round to throwing away. Although each little bit isn't much of a problem on its own, they build up to cause surprisingly large amounts of stress. You can never find anything, you're surrounded by mess . . . you always mean to do something about it but never quite find the time or the willpower. It means that you spend far more time doing things than you really need to because you can't find what you need, or can't face trying to look.

If this is you, then it's hard to emphasise just how worthwhile it would be to spend time sorting out the clutter.

Spend an afternoon going through your wardrobe. Throw away or donate to charity anything that you haven't worn in a year (unless you haven't worn it because you forgot it was there!). Put things together in an organised way – all work clothes together or all skirts/jumpers/jackets together. You'll know what will work best for you.

Spend an afternoon sorting out the tools or equipment in your workplace, if you have one. It will be much easier to get round to changing the plug you keep getting nagged about if you know where your screwdriver is.

Devote a day at work to going through your filing cabinet and throw away the papers from work or events that took place years ago and that you no longer really need. Make yourself create a proper filing system, either on paper or your computer, so that you know exactly where to find things you need.

Throw things away!

Don't tell yourself you don't have time because doing this will create quite amazing amounts of time once it's done. If you think you just can't face it, the following chapter offers some tips to help you stop putting things off.

11

Neat Tricks and Old Wisdom

Putting things off

Sometimes we know perfectly well what we need to do, but just can't make ourselves do it. We think of all sorts of excuses for putting things off! We can end up postponing things so much that they end up causing us more stress than if we'd bitten the bullet and done them in the first place.

One of the keys to understanding procrastination is to use your SATs record on pages 23–4, since it's often our thoughts that are causing us to procrastinate. These are thoughts that you need to dig down to get. For instance, if you've an essay to write or a report to finish, you might tell yourself that you're just waiting to get in the right mood, but in fact the truth may be: 'I won't be able to do it properly'; 'my tutor/boss will realise just how stupid I am, I won't be able to kid them any more'; 'I got an A last time and I was really pleased – what if I don't get one this time?' Often it's a more or less secret fear of failure that causes us to put things off – if we don't do it, at least we can't have failed at it. If this seems like you, then try using the following questioning and challenging techniques to combat the thoughts that are stopping you doing things. Ask yourself:

- Am I fortune telling? Am I assuming that I know how things will turn out when really I don't have a clue?

- Is there any evidence that things are going to go badly?

- What are the advantages of putting things off?

- What are the disadvantages of putting things off?

- Do the advantages of putting things off outweigh the disadvantages or the other way round?

Sometimes we do put things off because we're waiting to feel in the mood. Very often people believe that the chain of events goes like this:

Motivation
(feeling like doing something)

Action

In fact, if you wait to feel motivated to do something, you often won't. In reality, the links go like this:

Action

Motivation

If you can force yourself to start doing something, very often your motivation picks up, you start to feel more confident, and your capacity for action gets bigger.

You can experiment with this yourself. If you don't feel like doing something, make a start anyway, and see how you feel!

TICS and TOCS

'Oh no, I'm getting this all wrong.'

'I bet they're all thinking I'm a complete idiot.'

'There's no point doing this, there are so many other things I need to do that it won't make any difference.'

These are all examples of TICs – *task interfering cognitions*. These cognitions, or thoughts, crop up out of the blue when we're planning something, or when we're in the middle of something, and make it much more difficult for us. For example, if you're in an interview and start thinking, 'I bet they're all thinking I'm a complete idiot', you start to concentrate on feeling like an idiot, rather than on what you're being asked. You really will start to lose the thread, and your performance could well suffer. You can't think of two things at once! And you start to get more nervous and feel worse and worse, and this makes the TICs stronger.

So what we need to do is to swap these TICs for TOCs – *task orienting cognitions*. These are thoughts that help you to concentrate and to direct your attention to what is important in the situation, rather than yourself. Examples of these would be:

> 'I'll just ask him to repeat the question so I'm sure I know what he's asking.'

> 'I'll just take a moment to think it through before I answer.'

> 'Of course I can do it!'

> 'Concentrate!'

> 'Stop thinking about yourself, you chump!

If you know that you're going into a situation

where you're likely to have TICs, then spend a few moments preparing TOCs beforehand. When you're in the situation, you can just swap them as soon as you notice the TICs. But sometimes TICs will spring up on you before you know it and you can't think of any TOCs. If this happens, don't panic – you don't need TOCs to get rid of TICs. Just say, 'Oh, leave me alone, stupid TICs' or perhaps something a little more forceful! Dismiss the TICs – you don't have to think them – and go back to concentrating on what you need to do.

REMINDER

TICs are thoughts that appear from out of nowhere and **stop** us doing what we need to do. TOCs are thoughts that **motivate** us to do what we need to do.

Mindfulness and meditation

In our day-to-day lives, we rarely just think about what we're doing. In the middle of a meeting or class, we may be thinking about what we need to get from the supermarket, the argument we had with our partner that morning, how uncomfortable our trousers are . . .

Mindfulness sees that this style of thinking can be very harmful to us. It means that we're never fully engaged in what we're doing but are caught up in the stress and pain of things that have happened in the past, and things that may happen in the future. Instead, we should keep our minds on what we're doing at this moment, and not let ourselves drift to the past or the future. Instead we're choosing, on purpose, what we think about. In addition, we should pay attention to what we're doing and thinking without judging what is going on, or ourselves, or other people in the situation. There seems to be good evidence that people who manage to think in this way experience less stress.

REMINDER

Mindfulness means paying attention in a particular way:

- on purpose
- in the present moment
- without judging

First steps to mindfulness

Step 1: One very simple way in which you can keep mindful is to ask yourself – and answer – the following questions:

• Who am I? Myself

• Where am I? Here

• When is this? Now

These questions can be very helpful in directing your mind to the present moment.

Step 2: Mindfulness can also start with thinking about our breathing. Mostly we're not in touch with our breathing – it's just there, forgotten. We can start to be mindful by bringing our attention to our breath. Allow yourself ten minutes to go through the following exercise:

• Bring your attention to your breath, and let yourself be aware of all the physical sensations in your body as you breathe. You do not have to try to control the breath, just be aware of it.

• As you try to bring your attention to your breath you will find that other thoughts come into your mind. Do not trouble yourself about this, but just see that it has happened and return your attention to your breathing.

- As other thoughts come to you, imagine that your mind is like the sky. Your thoughts are like clouds that drift across the sky. They will come into your mind but you do not need to worry or judge them – just watch as the clouds enter and leave your field of vision, and bring your attention back to the breath.

Step 3: There are many other small things that you can do to stay in the present moment. Remember to use your body as a way to awareness. You're probably sitting as you read this. What are the sensations in your body at this moment? When you finish reading and stand up, feel the movements of standing, of walking to the next activity. Be 'in' your body as you move.

Step 4: Whenever you eat or drink something, take a moment and breathe. See your food, smell it, taste it, chew and swallow it. Look at the food and realise that it was connected to the earth, to the sunlight and rain.

Step 5: Whenever you bring your mind to the present, allow thoughts that come into your mind to drift through. Do not judge. Do not engage with these thoughts – just watch them.

The resourceful self

All of us have times when we cope well and other times when we can't cope – or feel that we can't – at all. When life seems difficult, it's easy to get stuck in the 'not coping' self and feel overwhelmed by what is going on around us or by our sense of inadequacy and failure. Nevertheless, we all carry within us our stronger or more resourceful self, who is there ready and waiting to come out! To get back to that self, think of a time when life was going well and you felt that you could manage. Think of a specific memory that your resourceful self was present in. Then ask yourself, 'What was I wearing? How was I carrying myself? What did I do and say?' Get a very specific, almost physical memory of how it felt. If you can't really remember anything, then let yourself imagine how you would like your resourceful self to be. Now step into the resourceful self, and let that self guide what you do and how you feel. You may be surprised at what you come up with!

12

A Final Word of Encouragement

This book provides information about stress and introduces you to strategies that have been shown to be effective in tackling stress. Because stress is such a complex condition, not everything in the book will suit everyone, but try to experiment with different strategies until you find those that suit you best. Remember that it can take a lot of practice to master some of the strategies – they are a skill like any other. Keep going, and the very best of luck!

Other Things that Might Help

If you've experienced some benefit from this book but would like to take it further, or if you feel that you need a different kind of approach, don't worry – self-help is not for everyone, and there are many other resources available.

Make an appointment to see your family doctor and ask about alternatives. You may benefit from medication, or more formal therapy. You may also benefit from some help with applying these strategies from a qualified psychologist or health worker, since self-help does work better if you have someone supporting you.

We also recommend the following self-help books:

The Compassionate Mind Approach to Reducing Stress by Maureen Cooper, published by Robinson (2013).

Mindfulness: A practical guide to finding peace in a frantic world by Mark Williams and Dr Danny Penman, published by Piatkus (2011).

Overcoming Stress by Lee Brosan and Gillian Todd, published by Robinson (2009).

How to Deal with Stress by Stephen Palmer and Cary Cooper, published by Kogan Page (2007).

The Mindful Way through Depression: Freeing Yourself from Chronic Unhappiness by Mark Williams, John Teasdale, Zindel Seal and Jon Kabat-Zinn, published by Guilford Press (2007). (Although focused on depression, it provides a good introduction to mindfulness, by authors world-famous for its development.)

The following organisations offer help and advice on stress and a range of common mental health issues, and you may find them a useful source of information.

British Association for Behavioural and Cognitive Psychotherapies
☎: 0161 705 4304
Email: babcp@babcp.com
Website: www.babcp.com

International Stress Management Association
Email: admin@isma.org.uk
Website: isma.org.uk